SUBMARINES

and Other Underwater Craft

727

SUBMARINES
and Other Underwater Craft

BY HARVEY WEISS

THOMAS Y. CROWELL   NEW YORK

ACKNOWLEDGMENTS

The author wishes to thank Master Chief Quartermaster Thomas J. Stebbins, U.S. Navy (retired), for his generous and expert advice on the preparation of this book. Illustrations have been made available by the United States Navy, the Submarine Force Library and Museum in Groton, Connecticut, and the Woods Hole Oceanographic Institute in Woods Hole, Massachusetts. The cover photograph is from the U.S. Navy.

SUBMARINES AND OTHER UNDERWATER CRAFT

Copyright © 1990 by Harvey Weiss
Printed in the U.S.A. All rights reserved.
Typography by Elynn Cohen
10 9 8 7 6 5 4 3 2 1
First Edition

Library of Congress Cataloging-in-Publication Data
Weiss, Harvey.
    Submarines and other underwater craft / Harvey Weiss.
        p.   cm.
    Summary: Describes the development and design refinements of
submarines, the different types, and their uses in such activities
as deep sea exploration and treasure hunting. Also discusses life
aboard a submarine.
    ISBN 0-690-04759-2 : $. — ISBN 0-690-04761-4 (lib. bdg.) :
$
    1. Submarine boats—Juvenile literature.   2. Submersibles—
Juvenile literature.   [1. Submarines.   2. Submarine boats.]
I. Title.
VM365.W45 1990   89-37614
359.3'257—dc20   CIP
                                                               AC

Contents

Introduction

The seas that cover seventy percent of our planet are a dark, deep, hidden world. In this undersea world there are unexplored canyons, shallow, treacherous reefs, underwater mountain ranges, and even erupting volcanoes. Marine life of all kinds exists—everything from tiny coral animals to colossal whales. Even today this world is only partly explored.

The submarines that travel these sometimes dangerous depths are a wonder of modern science. The submarine has developed over the last hundred years from the simplest, crudest vessel into a machine that is fast, sleek, and very efficient. Today submarines are nuclear-powered and able to cruise around the world without surfacing even once.

It is rather sad, but one of the reasons that the submarine has become such a powerful, beautifully engineered machine is because of its use in times of war. As we shall see as we look at the different kinds of submarines, much of their development occurred in order to create the most deadly weapon possible.

However, all submarines aren't for purposes of war. There are many kinds of deep-water exploratory craft: scientific-research submarines, diving bells, and undersea, remote-control vessels. They are used to chart the ocean, search for new kinds of marine life, maintain drilling platforms and similar underwater structures, and even search for sunken treasure.

This is a very small submarine that is used for all sorts of scientific deep-sea research. This one is named the *Alvin*, and some of its adventures are described later on in this book.

How a Submarine Works

A submarine is a boat. What makes it different from other boats is its ability to sink below the surface of the water and then come back up on command. A submarine that can sink and not resurface is in trouble! (There is an account on page 45 of just this sort of thing happening.)

This question of floating or not floating is a question of buoyancy. And buoyancy must be understood if you are to understand how a submarine operates.

Buoyancy

The basic rule of buoyancy is that anything will float if its weight is less than that of an equal volume of water. Let's take a specific case. Suppose you had a block of wood that measured one foot by one foot by one foot. That is one cubic foot. If this piece of wood was oak it would weigh fifty-three pounds. Now let us assume you could have a block of water the same volume—one cubic foot. It would weigh sixty-four pounds. That is what a cubic foot of water weighs. The block of wood and the block of water are the

The water weighs more than the wood. Therefore the wood will float.

53 pounds   64 pounds

hollow cubic foot of iron, 60 pounds

cubic foot of iron, 448 pounds

same volume—but the water is heavier. Therefore the wood will float.

What would happen if we had a cubic foot of iron? It would weigh 448 pounds. This is a lot heavier than an equal volume of water, so it would most certainly sink. How could we make it float? The only way would be to reduce its weight. And the only way to do that would be to hollow it out.

If we got its weight down to sixty pounds, that hollow block of iron would float. (As the rule says: Anything will float if its weight is less than an equal volume of water.)

If this hollow iron cube was a submarine and we wanted it to sink, we would have to increase its weight. If we could open it up for a moment, drop in five pounds of pebbles, then seal it up tight again, it would sink. It would now weigh sixty-five pounds, and an equal volume of water is only sixty-four pounds.

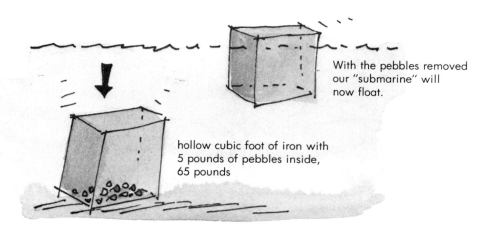

With the pebbles removed our "submarine" will now float.

hollow cubic foot of iron with 5 pounds of pebbles inside, 65 pounds

If we wanted our "submarine" to rise up to the surface again we would have to remove those five pounds of pebbles.

But in a real submarine there aren't a lot of pebbles to add or remove. There is another kind of weight, however, that is much more available and very easy to manage—water! A real submarine will take in water, or pump out water, in order to sink or float. All submarines work on this principle. Every submarine has tanks that are part of the hull. And water can be pumped into or out of these tanks in order to change the buoyancy of the submarine. When the water is pumped out of these tanks, they will fill with air, which is much lighter than water.

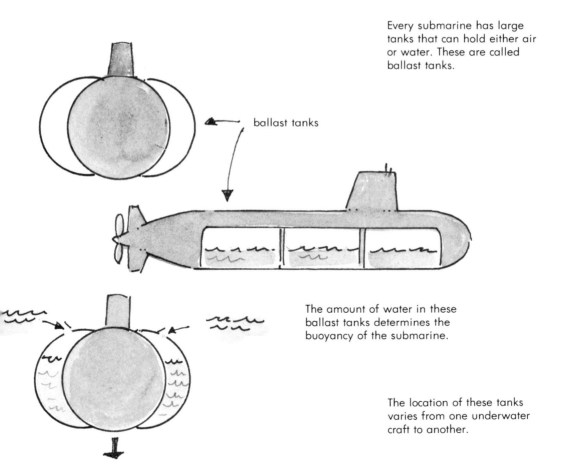

Every submarine has large tanks that can hold either air or water. These are called ballast tanks.

ballast tanks

The amount of water in these ballast tanks determines the buoyancy of the submarine.

The location of these tanks varies from one underwater craft to another.

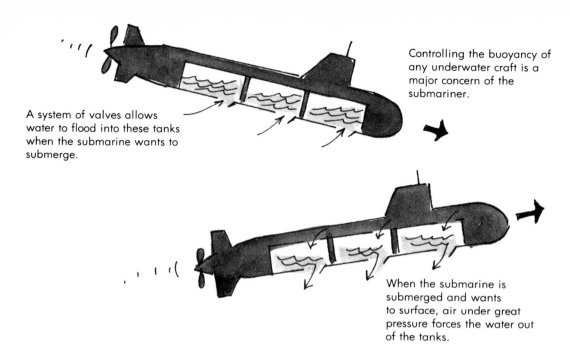

A system of valves allows water to flood into these tanks when the submarine wants to submerge.

Controlling the buoyancy of any underwater craft is a major concern of the submariner.

When the submarine is submerged and wants to surface, air under great pressure forces the water out of the tanks.

This water—or pebbles—is called ballast. Ballast is weight that can be added or removed in order for a submarine to change its buoyancy. It is what will cause the submarine to float or sink.

Submarines are dealing with buoyancy all the time. There are three kinds of buoyancy:

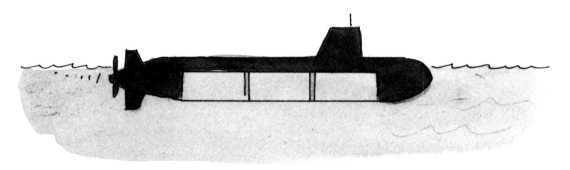

1. positive buoyancy—the submarine floats on the surface.

2. negative buoyancy—weight (ballast) has been added so the submarine sinks below the surface.

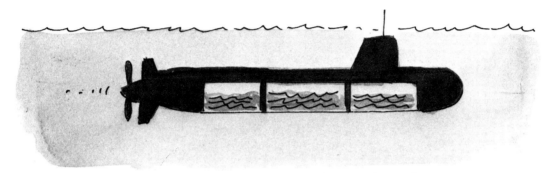

3. neutral buoyancy—this is a delicate balance between negative and positive buoyancy. In this condition the submarine can remain below the surface of the water without sinking any deeper, and it can travel about underwater without moving either up or down.

If a submarine has neutral buoyancy it can be made to head up or down by means of diving fins as shown below. If the submarine is moving forward at some speed and the fins are angled as shown, the submarine will head down. Frequently this method of changing depth is used instead of altering the ballast.

These fins (called diving planes) are located in various places on different submarines. They can be placed at the stern as shown here, or near the bow, or almost anywhere else.

First Attempts

The idea of an underwater boat intrigued many inventors in early times. Many years ago one French inventor imagined an underwater railroad using a submarine on wheels. It was supposed to run along a track laid under the English Channel between France and England. If there was a need for some fresh air, or a sudden urge to do some fishing, the submarine could surface. Then, after a while, it would submerge back onto the tracks and continue on its way. Like many farfetched schemes, this looked pretty good on paper but wasn't very practical.

Another inventor designed a submarine with a large steam-powered drill mounted on the top of the vessel. The idea was to come up under an enemy warship and drill holes in the bottom. Then, with luck, the submarine would be able to duck away from under the sinking enemy boat!

Another, rather gloomy inventor thought of a submarine that would be divided into three parts. If there was an accident or injury to one part of the submarine, that part would be detached and left behind. The other two parts would be joined together and then continue on their way. Hopefully, none of the crew would be left behind in the abandoned third of this submarine.

Many inventors—or would-be inventors—came up with all sorts of wild ideas about submarines. The idea of traveling about underwater was intriguing, but the technology of the times was not up to it. It wasn't until the latter part of the nineteenth century, as we will see, that the first really practical submarine came to be.

The *Turtle*

The *Turtle* was a rather impractical, but historically interesting, submarine. It is an odd-looking craft. In fact, it doesn't look like any kind of boat at all, much less like a submarine. It looks more like a turnip. However, the inventor must have thought it looked like a turtle, because that is what he named it.

The *Turtle* is important in the history of submarines, because it was the first submarine to submerge by filling its tanks with water. And it was the first to travel underwater to attack another vessel. All this in 1776!

The *Turtle* was built by David Bushnell, a bright young graduate of Yale University. The *Turtle* no longer exists, but we have a very clear idea of what it was like because Bushnell described it quite carefully in a letter he wrote to Thomas Jefferson.

A paragraph in his letter to Jefferson explains how the *Turtle* could be made to sink below the surface of the water: "When the operator would descend, he placed his foot upon the top of a brass valve, depressing it by which he opened a large aperture in the bottom of the vessel, through which water entered at his pleasure; when he had admitted a sufficient quantity he descended very gradually; if he admitted too much he ejected as much as was necessary to obtain an equilibrium by the two forcing pumps which were placed at each hand. Whenever the vessel leaked, or he would ascend to the surface, he also made use of these forcing pumps. When the skillful operator had obtained equilibrium he could row upward or downward, or continue at any particular depth with an

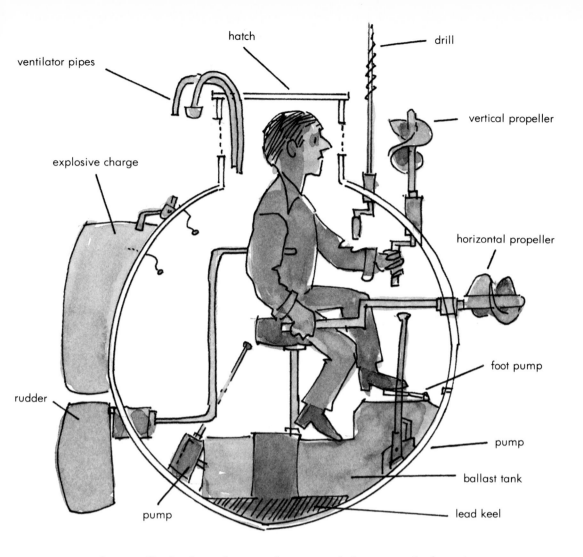

ventilator pipes

hatch

drill

vertical propeller

explosive charge

horizontal propeller

rudder

foot pump

pump

ballast tank

pump

lead keel

oar [propeller] placed near the top of the vessel, forming up on the principle of the screw, the axis of the oar entering the vessel; by turning the oar one way he raised the vessel; by turning it the other way he depressed it." Some of this explanation may seem a bit awkward, but if you look at the drawing above you'll be able to understand just how the *Turtle* worked.

Bushnell built his vessel and tested it carefully until he was satisfied with its performance. The army then provided a volunteer to operate it in what was the first submarine war mission—an attack on an enemy warship. As it turned out, the mission was a quite dramatic adventure.

The *Turtle* Attacks

It started on September 6th, 1776, with Sergeant Ezra Lee in charge. (Sergeant Lee was the crew as well as captain because the *Turtle* had room for just one person.)

The *Turtle* was towed at night to a point upriver from where the British fleet was anchored in New York Harbor. The *Turtle* was released and allowed to drift down the river with the outgoing tide, toward the British fleet. However, the tide was stronger than expected, and the *Turtle* was carried past the British moorings. Sergeant Lee had to crank the *Turtle* back up against the tide until it reached the British *Eagle,* a ship of considerable size, mounting sixty-four guns.

Finally submerged in position beneath the *Eagle,* Sergeant Lee tried to drill into the bottom of the wood hull. The tool bit (the twisted cutting end of the drill—like a screw) was supposed to screw into the hull of the *Eagle* and hold explosives in place. But Lee couldn't manage to do it. Nobody knows why he failed. It may have been that he struck an iron fastening and couldn't drill through it. Or maybe he was just so weak from his exertions and lack of oxygen that he didn't have the strength to do the job. In any case he gave up, came to the surface, and headed back upstream. Unfortunately, a British guard boat saw him and gave chase.

When he saw that the British were coming after him, he set the fuse on his explosives and let them float off

The *Turtle* had a difficult time trying to drill into the hull of the British *Eagle*.

behind him. When they exploded with great violence a few moments later, the British decided that it might be wiser not to pursue this strange vessel any farther. And Sergeant Ezra Lee was able to get away unharmed, but, we may assume, was a very exhausted young man. That was the first—and last—mission of the *Turtle*.

Keeping the Peace

Many of the engineers and inventors who worked with submarines did so because they thought submarines might be a way to prevent wars. They thought of themselves as peacemakers rather than "war merchants." They believed that if you have the most deadly weapons at your disposal, no enemies are going to start a war because they will know that you have more powerful weapons than they do. (A submarine built in 1885 was, in fact, called the *Peacemaker*!)

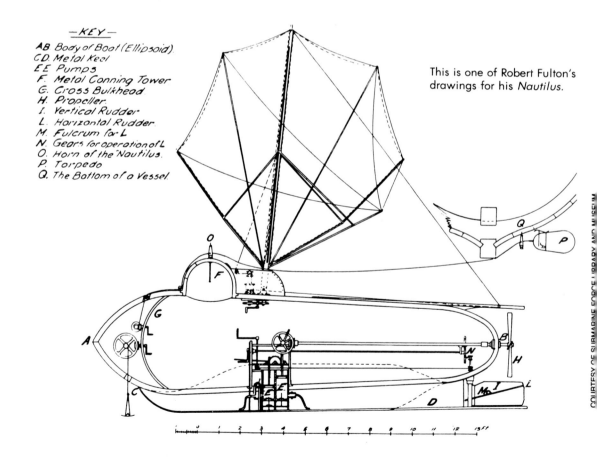

—KEY—

AB. Body of Boat (Ellipsoid).
CD. Metal Keel
EE. Pumps
F. Metal Conning Tower
G. Cross Bulkhead
H. Propeller.
I. Vertical Rudder
L. Horizontal Rudder.
M. Fulcrum for L
N. Gears for operation of L
O. Horn of the Nautilus.
P. Torpedo
Q. The Bottom of a Vessel.

This is one of Robert Fulton's drawings for his *Nautilus*.

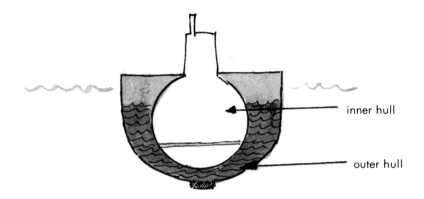

inner hull

outer hull

This is a cross-sectional view of Fulton's submarine. There was an inner hull for the crew and an outer hull that served as a ballast tank. The ballast tank was flooded to submerge. The water was pumped out when it was time to surface.

Robert Fulton, who was born in 1775, was an ardent pacifist. He violently hated the idea of war. Fulton is best known for using a steam engine to propel a boat, but he also gave a lot of thought to submarines. He believed submarines would make all warships obsolete, and then there would be peace, free trade among nations, and freedom of the seas.

In 1800 he built a submarine called the *Nautilus*. There was room for three people in it, and there was a conning tower and diving planes. (A conning tower is a raised section on the hull from which a submarine can be controlled.) The *Nautilus* carried explosives that could be attached to the bottom of a warship. It was propelled by a hand-turned propeller and had a rather odd kite-shaped sail that could be raised when the submarine was on the surface.

Fulton spent much time and effort trying to get the *Nautilus* adopted by various governments, including the Dutch, English, and French. But nobody was interested, and Fulton finally gave up his dream of a peacemaking submarine.

Power

Inventors in many countries were trying to build a practical, workable submarine during the late 1800s. But there was one major drawback: There existed no practical means of propulsion. There was no simple, dependable engine that could fit inside a submarine. Without an engine a submarine can't travel fast or far. A hand-cranked propeller like that used on the *Turtle* wasn't very practical. It took a lot of manpower, was very tedious, and was not very efficient.

During this period the steam engine was coming into general use. It had already been used to pump water out of deep mine shafts, to power trains, and to run various kinds of factory machinery. Robert Fulton, the designer of the *Nautilus*, was building an efficient steamboat. Inventors decided to try a steam-powered submarine.

A steam engine is rather small and compact and can fit neatly into even a small submarine. But the boiler that provides the steam to operate the engine is another matter altogether. This is a clumsy, bulky affair with tubes, a fire chamber, and a metal shell able to withstand the stress of high-pressure steam. And there is another drawback: Smoke from the fire and exhaust from the engine require a smokestack that has to remain above water when the engine is in use.

A steam-propelled submarine worked fine when it was on the surface. But as soon as it was submerged the fire had to be dampened or put out, and the smokestack had to be closed up and folded down out of the way. And with the steam engine not working, the submarine had

As you can see, a steam engine with boiler would be a rather clumsy and bulky affair to squeeze into a submarine.

to have some alternate means of propulsion while submerged. All this turned out to be slow, clumsy, and quite impractical.

When the electric motor was developed in the early 1900s, the submarine found the ideal means of propulsion. Now the submarine could travel underwater at a good speed for several hours. The electric motor produced no exhaust and was small and reliable. The batteries that

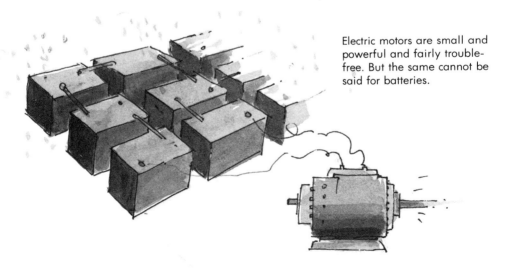

Electric motors are small and powerful and fairly trouble-free. But the same cannot be said for batteries.

provided the electricity for the motor were more of a problem, however. These were heavy, and a great many of them were needed to power the electric motor. They took up a lot of space, and they lost their energy after a few hours of use and had to be recharged. They were also dangerous and gave off poisonous fumes if any seawater got into them.

The acid used in batteries was also dangerous. A 1905 booklet offering guidance to naval officers in submarines had this to say: "If you get covered with strong acid it is a good idea to jump overboard and stay there till the doctor is ready." We must assume that this advice refers to an accidental acid spill while the submarine is on the surface and not going anywhere!

John P. Holland

The problems with steam engines or with batteries running out of energy were neatly solved by an American submarine designer. His name was John P. Holland and he built a submarine that used a gasoline engine. This sort

Here the gasoline engine is connected directly to the generator, which is charging the batteries. However, it was also possible to connect the engine directly to the submarine's propeller when traveling on the surface.

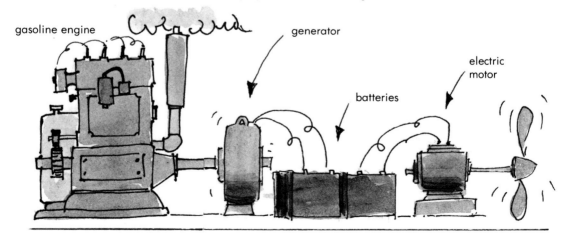

gasoline engine · · · · · · · · · · · · generator

electric motor

batteries

This is a famous photograph of Mr. Holland looking his most distinguished in a fancy bowler hat and striped tie, with a very elegant moustache. He is standing in the hatch of one of his submarines.

of motor was lightweight, not too bulky, and could turn the propeller. It could also be used to run a generator. (A generator is a machine that generates electricity.) This electricity could be used to charge batteries, and it would no longer be necessary to return to port to get them charged. This gave the submarine much more freedom of action.

Why bother with batteries to drive an electric motor if there was a gasoline engine available? The reason is that the gasoline engine cannot be used while the submarine is submerged. A gasoline engine needs lots of air to "breathe," and there is also the problem of removing the exhaust fumes from the submarine. Thus when the submarine was submerged, the electric motor had to be used.

Holland had been building submarines for several years and had established a reputation as an expert in this field. In 1898 the United States government ordered a submarine from Mr. Holland. It wasn't a great success because the

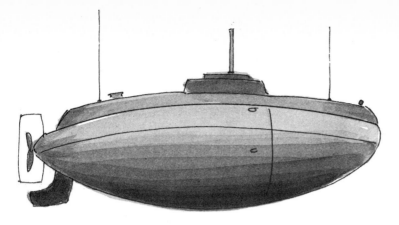

This is the U.S. Navy's first submarine—the *USS Holland*—which was launched in 1898. It was a rather slow-moving, stubby vessel, but it worked well and was the basis for later, improved, more efficient models.

navy insisted on many changes of which Holland didn't approve. Another submarine, built to Holland's standards, was then built and bought by the government in 1900.

It was called the *USS Holland*. (Mr. Holland wasn't about to let anybody forget that he was the man responsible for this vessel.) It is considered the first really successful, practical submarine. It contained many of the ideas and methods that are still used in modern submarines. It was 53 feet 10 inches long and 10 feet 3 inches in diameter, and weighed 64 tons. It had "saddle tanks," built around the outside of the hull, which held the water ballast. When the tanks were filled with sea water, the *USS Holland* weighed 74 tons. The maximum depth to which the *USS Holland* could dive was 100 feet.

An improvement over the gasoline engine that Holland used was developed several years later. It was the diesel engine. It is quiet, efficient, and uses a less explosive fuel. Diesel engines are still used in some of the old, non-nuclear submarines. Like the gasoline engine, however, it cannot be used when the submarine is submerged. At this time batteries and an electric motor must be used.

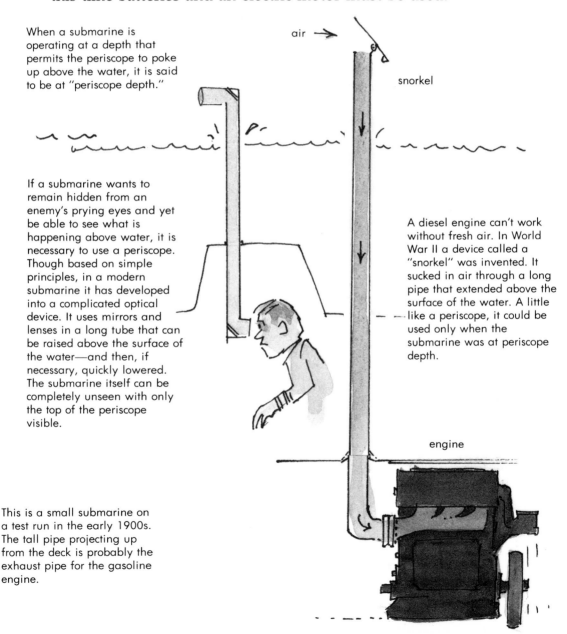

When a submarine is operating at a depth that permits the periscope to poke up above the water, it is said to be at "periscope depth."

air →

snorkel

If a submarine wants to remain hidden from an enemy's prying eyes and yet be able to see what is happening above water, it is necessary to use a periscope. Though based on simple principles, in a modern submarine it has developed into a complicated optical device. It uses mirrors and lenses in a long tube that can be raised above the surface of the water—and then, if necessary, quickly lowered. The submarine itself can be completely unseen with only the top of the periscope visible.

A diesel engine can't work without fresh air. In World War II a device called a "snorkel" was invented. It sucked in air through a long pipe that extended above the surface of the water. A little like a periscope, it could be used only when the submarine was at periscope depth.

engine

This is a small submarine on a test run in the early 1900s. The tall pipe projecting up from the deck is probably the exhaust pipe for the gasoline engine.

Submarines at War

The first weapon used by a submarine was a drill—the weapon used by the *Turtle* in 1776. It wasn't much of a weapon, but if it had been successful it would have attached an explosive charge and blown a hole in the bottom of the British *Eagle*.

During the Civil War the Confederate army (there was no navy to speak of) built a man-powered submarine that had an explosive charge attached to the end of a long pole that was attached to the front of the submarine. This kind

a spar torpedo

of weapon was called a spar torpedo, and it often did as much damage to the attacking vessel as to the one being attacked. The Confederate submarine was called the *Hunley*—the name of the designer—and from the very beginning it was a bad-luck vessel. It was propelled by eight men turning a crankshaft that turned the propeller. It sank once when a large wave came through the open hatch, swamping the boat and drowning most of the hardworking crew. The vessel was hauled up to be used again, but

This is a drawing of the *Hunley* made by a man who was one of the builders of the submarine.

it finally came to a disastrous end when it charged the northern warship the mighty *Housatonic*. The 143 pounds of explosives in the spar torpedo blew a huge hole in the enemy ship, which promptly heeled over and sank. This was the first warship actually sunk by a submarine. But, unfortunately, the *Hunley*, with its crew, also sank. Years later, underwater explorers found the remains of the *Hunley* inside the *Housatonic*. The theory is that the suction of the larger ship going down sucked the *Hunley* into the large hole that had been blasted in its side.

Torpedoes

The torpedo was the first accurate and deadly submarine weapon. Early in World War I the power of torpedoes was demonstrated when a German submarine encountered three British cruisers and sank them all. Fourteen hundred fifty-nine men died in this attack, and it suddenly became clear that submarines and their torpedoes were a very serious threat.

On early submarines the torpedoes were attached to the outside of the hull. Aiming the torpedo was done by aiming the entire submarine. But this method was rarely accurate. Torpedoes fell off by accident or went in the wrong direction, or the submarine itself wasn't correctly aimed. Eventually torpedo tubes were used, and this is the method that is used today. A torpedo tube is like the barrel of a gun, but the "gun" doesn't have to be aimed directly at the target because there are various methods of directing the way the torpedo travels once it is on its way to its target.

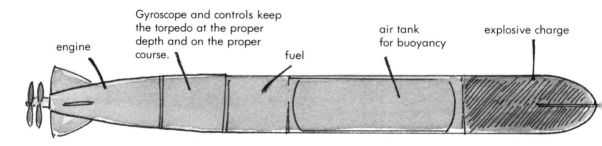

engine

Gyroscope and controls keep the torpedo at the proper depth and on the proper course.

fuel

air tank for buoyancy

explosive charge

A torpedo is a complicated weapon. It must contain an explosive charge, an engine to make it go, and some kind of guidance system to keep it on course and at the proper depth. It is important that the torpedo travel at the right distance below the surface. Too deep and it might go under the target; too high and it might be seen approaching, enabling evasive action.

The first torpedoes were propelled by engines that were run by compressed air. But today there are many other types, including electric motor and piston engines using

In wartime some ships use torpedo nets or extra armor to protect against torpedoes.

Even though aimed accurately, a torpedo that is not running at the proper depth will miss its target.

a variety of fuels. The modern torpedoes have all kinds of devices to help them get to the target. Some devices cause the torpedo to home in on the noise, or heat, or magnetic field produced by the hull of an enemy ship. There are other torpedoes that trail a wire as they move through the water. Signals from the submarine pass through the wire, guiding the torpedo on its way.

Anti-Submarine Warfare

Submarines are not only attackers, they are also targets. Enemy forces will do their very best to destroy them. Destroyers and other surface craft carry depth charges intended for just this purpose. Depth charges are explosive devices that are set to explode at various depths. If one is dropped and hits a submarine—or comes close— the force of the explosion will crush the hull.

The depth charge must be set to go off at the proper depth. If it goes off much above or below the submarine, no serious damage will be caused.

The undersea mines used in World Wars I and II were set off by actual contact with a submarine. Some modern mines, however, don't have to actually be struck in order to go off—just getting close is enough.

Undersea mines are another hazard. These are weapons similar to depth charges. However, they are anchored to the sea bottom at various depths. A submarine that bumps into or even comes near one of these mines will probably be destroyed.

Submarines are also in trouble if they are caught on the surface. Older submarines had to surface in order to charge their batteries, and in doing so became easy targets for attack by enemy airplanes or warships. Submarine captains used to wait until night or for rainy weather before surfacing to charge their batteries.

The submarines that the German navy used during World Wars I and II were called U-boats. The "U" stands for *Untersee*, or undersea. All kinds of anti-submarine methods were used by the British and the Americans to keep the U-boats from sinking Allied ships. The defense most used was the convoy. Many merchant cargo ships—sometimes fifty or more—were huddled together and guarded by a few destroyers and perhaps a cruiser or two. This wasn't foolproof protection, but it did drastically cut down on the number of sinkings.

Minisubs were used with much success in World War II. Anchored warships and supply ships were favorite targets for these small, secretive submarines.

Very small submarines were built by several different countries during World War II. Anti-submarine defenses were not very good against such small vessels. Some of them had three- or four-man crews and were like miniature submarines. Others were the size of a torpedo and the crew sat astride them, almost like riding a bicycle. These midget submarines could get into small harbors and other well-defended anchorages without being detected. Some of them carried torpedoes, but many others carried explosive charges that were attached to the undersides of enemy ships—just as the *Turtle* tried to do in 1776. These explosive charges were timed to go off after the midget submarine had left the scene.

Hide and Seek

A submarine that can be located by an enemy is in trouble. A submarine has no defense against depth charges or torpedoes coming at it from another submarine. The only real protection a submarine has is its stealth and silence. If a submarine can't be found, it can't be attacked.

The best way to locate a submerged submarine is with a detection device called "sonar," which stands for "sound navigation and ranging." Sonar works on the same principle as radar. A sound signal is sent out through the water. If the signal strikes an object such as a submarine, it will echo or bounce back to the sender. The distance

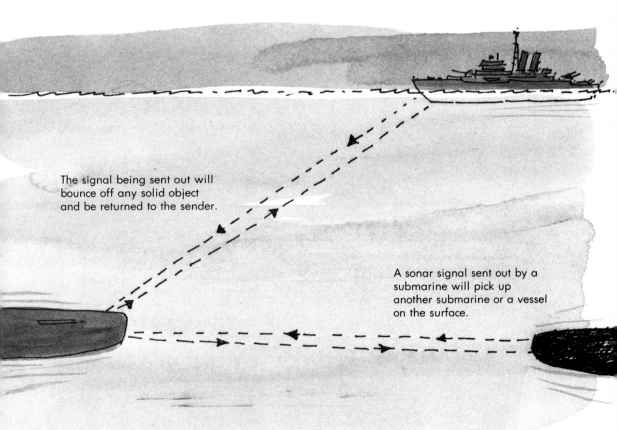

The signal being sent out will bounce off any solid object and be returned to the sender.

A sonar signal sent out by a submarine will pick up another submarine or a vessel on the surface.

and direction this signal has traveled can be very accurately computed. Sonar is used on surface ships that are hunting for submarines. It is also used on submarines that are searching for surface ships or other submarines.

Sonar is a kind of "super ear." It is able to pick up sound produced by anything on or in the water. The sound of a turning propeller from another submarine or a destroyer can be detected from far away. It is even possible with modern equipment to recognize and identify the particular vessel by the sound of its propeller or the noise from machinery that is running as it moves through the water.

When a submarine is trying to hide, complete silence is ordered on board, conversation carried on only in whispers. Sometimes the crew even take off their shoes and move about in stocking feet. And if somebody is clumsy enough to drop a tool or slam down a pot in the galley—is he in trouble!

The Nuclear-Powered Submarine

Before the development of the nuclear-powered submarine, movement underwater was completely dependent on batteries. The usual practice was for the submarine to surface at night and recharge the batteries for the next day's operations. The submarine commander watched the condition of his batteries with the utmost attention. If they were low, the skipper would never go on the offensive, even when the juiciest target was close by. He knew he had limited power for fast maneuvering or for a speedy retreat if the batteries were not fully charged.

A bright, young navy captain named Hyman Rickover knew how dependent the submarines were on batteries, and how this limited their effectiveness. He also knew all about nuclear power. He became convinced that a nuclear propulsion system would be perfect for submarines. A nuclear-powered submarine would not need oil or gasoline or batteries. A nuclear reactor would produce enough power to keep the submarine going for a half million miles. It could stay underwater almost indefinitely.

The Atomic Energy Commission, which controlled all nuclear research, wasn't very interested in submarine development. It was concerned only with building bigger and better explosive devices—bombs of almost inconceivable power—and nuclear power plants. But with great energy and determination Rickover finally managed to

How a Nuclear Reactor Works

This is a very simplified plan of a nuclear-power system of the sort found on a nuclear submarine.

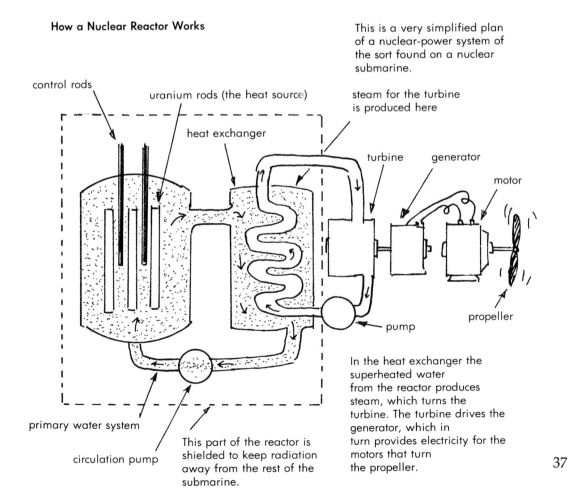

control rods

uranium rods (the heat source)

heat exchanger

steam for the turbine is produced here

turbine   generator

motor

primary water system

circulation pump

pump

propeller

This part of the reactor is shielded to keep radiation away from the rest of the submarine.

In the heat exchanger the superheated water from the reactor produces steam, which turns the turbine. The turbine drives the generator, which in turn provides electricity for the motors that turn the propeller.

37

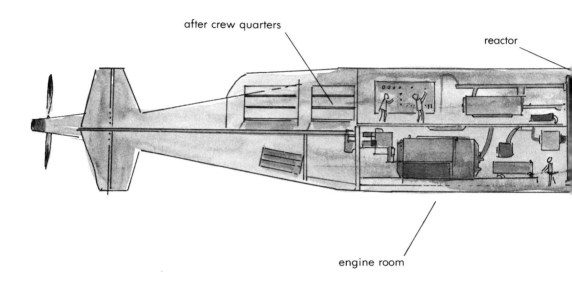

The *Nautilus* is 319 feet long
with a beam (width) of 27 feet.

after crew quarters

reactor

engine room

convince the navy and the Atomic Energy Commission that nuclear power was possible and indeed the ideal propulsion method for submarines.

On January 17, 1955, the first nuclear-powered submarine, the *Nautilus* (named after many earlier submarines with this name), proceeded out to sea and proved to be a complete and dramatic success. The *Nautilus* was able to travel enormous distances without surfacing. On her very first voyage, the *Nautilus* traveled completely submerged some 1,300 miles from her home port in New London, Connecticut, to Puerto Rico. This was an amazing feat at that time. It was a greater distance than any

The speed and power of a nuclear-powered submarine are evident in this photograph. The figures on the bridge will give an idea of the size of this vessel.

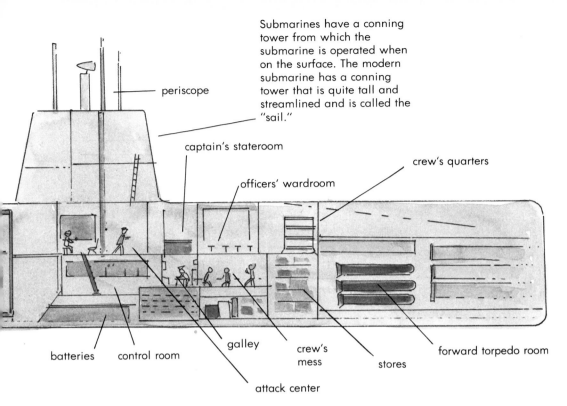

Submarines have a conning tower from which the submarine is operated when on the surface. The modern submarine has a conning tower that is quite tall and streamlined and is called the "sail."

periscope

captain's stateroom

officers' wardroom

crew's quarters

batteries

control room

galley

crew's mess

stores

forward torpedo room

attack center

submarine had ever traveled while submerged. In 1958 the *Nautilus* traveled under the polar ice cap and reached the North Pole. The following year another nuclear submarine traveled underwater for three months without once "coming up for air." From this time on very few submarines were built anywhere in the world that were not powered by nuclear energy.

This meeting of two United States nuclear-powered submarines took place near the North Pole in 1962.

A nautilus is a seashell that has an interesting spiral shape. It is a name that is important to mariners because it has a long tradition. In the Jules Verne science fiction novel *20,000 Leagues Under the Sea* there is a wonderful underwater craft called the *Nautilus* that is the center of many exciting adventures. This same name—*Nautilus*—has, over the years, been given to quite a few United States navy submarines.

Missiles

The most deadly weapons in existence are carried in nuclear-powered submarines. Intercontinental missiles that can travel for thousands of miles—from one continent to another—can be fired off while a submarine is completely submerged. The missile is shot up through the water by compressed air. Then, when the missile is sixty or so feet above the surface, the motor ignites and the missile goes on its way to the target.

The U.S. navy has a Trident class of submarines. These are nuclear-powered submarines that carry either sixteen or twenty-four Trident missiles. Each of these missiles has several warheads, each one capable of destroying a medium-sized city! (The warhead is that part of the missile that is detachable and contains the nuclear explosive.) One submarine with its missiles has more explosive power than the explosives used in all of World War II. The purpose of this class of submarine is to cruise about, whereabouts unknown, hidden under the water and ready at a moment's notice to send the missiles on their deadly way. This kind of submarine might be called a "deterrent submarine," because its purpose is to serve as a threat. It is a way to deter aggression. It says "Don't hit me, because I have something mighty big to hit back with!"

This is the nuclear-powered strategic missile submarine *USS Ohio*. This type of submarine will spend most of its time submerged, carrying its load of deadly weapons, its whereabouts known to only a few.

Life Aboard a Submarine

A submarine will never have the space and comfort found on a battleship or aircraft carrier. But life aboard a modern nuclear submarine is a lot better than aboard the early diesel-electric ones. In those old boats the bunks were small and fitted into odd, leftover spaces. They were so small, in fact, that a man could hardly turn over. If he wanted to turn over, he usually had to get out of the bunk, then crawl back in facing the other way. And chances were that his bunk would be wedged in between two torpedoes, or fitted in next to some clammy piece of mechanical equipment.

There are stories that World War I submariners could be smelled as they approached from some way off. The odor of fuel oil, many people tightly packed in small space, poor ventilation, and not many showers produced a most distinctive odor. It could only be removed, over a period of time, with the most vigorous and lengthy scrubbing. There still are no bathtubs, grand pianos, or overstuffed sofas aboard the modern submarine, but life is a lot more comfortable than it used to be.

Work aboard a submarine is constant and intensive, and no crew can keep it up without a break. Rather than leave the submarine idle while the crew has a chance to rest, a system of using two crews for each submarine has been developed. One crew is called the blue and the other the gold. When one crew leaves the submarine—usually after sixty days—the other crew takes over.

The control room, which is the heart of the submarine, is fairly roomy and comfortable so that the crew can work with the greatest attention and concentration.

In all submarines there is a tradition of the very best food, cooked with care and skill. There are also a small library, films, courses in various subjects, and all kinds of music on tape.

Disasters

One of the most sudden and tragic submarine disasters occurred in 1963 with the nuclear submarine *Thresher*. This multimillion-dollar submarine was on a shakedown cruise following repairs and modifications. She was accompanied by a companion ship that stayed in communication with the *Thresher* as it went down toward 1,000 feet in a test dive. The *Thresher* never came up. The last words heard were in a garbled message including the words "test depth." "Test depth" is the lowest depth to which a submarine can safely go. It is not clear if the message was saying that the test depth had been reached or if the *Thresher* was sinking below the test depth and headed for trouble.

There were 129 men lost in this accident, and the hull was never recovered. The ocean where the *Thresher* went down was over 8,000 feet deep. At this depth the water pressure is enormous and this made rescue efforts impossible. But the fact is there was no submarine to rescue. The water pressure was so great it simply crushed the *Thresher* as it went lower and lower until it finally imploded (exploded inward). Photographs show bits and pieces of the submarine scattered over the ocean floor. The only piece of the *Thresher* that was brought to the surface was a twisted piece of brass pipe. No bodies were ever seen or recovered.

There was a lengthy official hearing after this accident to try and determine its cause. The most logical opinion is that a major pipe in the hull had broken, allowing a violent inrush of water and general flooding. Once the submarine descended below the test depth she was designed for, the hull shattered. There was no way the hull of the *Thresher* could resist the pressure of the water much below the 1,000-foot test depth. At 8,400 feet the pressure is approximately two tons per square inch, and that is a great deal more than any submarine can withstand.

Various kinds of rescue devices have been developed over the years. The one shown here is a large, bell-like air chamber that can be lowered onto a special rescue hatch on the deck of the submarine. When a watertight attachment has been made, the hatch is opened and the crew can climb into the "bell" and be hoisted to the surface.

Another major submarine casualty was the case of the *Scorpion*. Two hundred fifty-two feet long with a crew of ninety-nine officers and men, the *Scorpion* simply disappeared in 1968. After an extensive search, portions of the hull were located under more than 10,000 feet of water. Nobody knows what happened.

But accidents aboard submarines are few and far between. Every part in a modern submarine is built with care and skill and of the very finest materials. Everything is constantly checked, rechecked, and then checked again, so the chance of anything not performing as intended is very unlikely. Submariners feel that it is as safe to travel deep underwater in a submarine as it is to travel across town by bus.

Pressure

Pressure is one of the biggest concerns of the submariner. The human body is always under pressure. The air that surrounds you constantly presses against your body. Underwater it is the water that presses against you. Water is a lot heavier than air and therefore presses much harder.

Imagine a pail of water resting on your chest. It might be a bit uncomfortable, but it wouldn't cause any real harm. But now imagine ten pails of water, one piled on top of the other, sitting on your chest. This would create a weight or pressure that would be very uncomfortable indeed, and perhaps quite harmful. If you were a diver or a submarine under water "ten pails" deep, this kind of pressure would be not only on your chest, but pressing in from all directions—sides, top, and bottom.

The deeper anything goes under the water, the more the pressure on it. At only 200 feet the pressure is ninety pounds pressing on each square inch of surface. At a depth of 8,500 feet the pressure is about two tons per square inch. One of the deepest dives on record (not in a submarine, but in a very heavy, hollow steel ball), was 35,800 feet. That is almost seven miles deep and there was a pressure of more than seven tons per square inch.

There is a term that submarine designers use when planning the strength of a hull. It is "collapse depth," which means the depth at which the water pressure will crush the submarine's hull. A submarine that is not too ruggedly built or not intended for great depths might have a collapse depth of 100 feet. A large, stronger nuclear submarine might have a collapse depth of 1,000 feet.

Getting About Underwater

Although a submarine can travel long distances underwater and dive deep, there are many jobs that it can't comfortably handle. Many tasks are small in scale and require the use of hands. For example, a submarine won't do you any good if you want to go spear fishing, or if you have to repair an underwater valve on an oil platform, or if you want to carefully explore a delicate coral reef. What is needed is a one-man "submarine" that can move freely about and that has hands—some kind of diver!

There is a simple device that will let a swimmer breathe with the head underwater. It is called a snorkel. It is a way to draw in fresh air by means of a curved pipe. One end is held in the mouth; the other end is kept above water. Flippers and a face mask are almost always used

the snorkel

The flippers are made of rubber—wear them on land and you will feel like a duck waddling about. But in the water they will easily double your swimming speed. The mask makes seeing easier.

with the snorkel. The mask makes seeing underwater easier, and the flippers increase speed and power enormously. This is, however, not a method for deep diving.

Scuba diving is quite different from swimming about with a snorkel. The word "scuba" stands for "self-contained underwater breathing apparatus." A scuba diver carries the air to breathe in a tank or tanks strapped on his back and can therefore remain underwater for a considerable amount of time. The air from the tank goes through a hose and then through a device called a regulator and then into the mouth. The regulator controls the amount of air and the pressure at which it is delivered. The scuba diver must be thoroughly trained because the misuse of this equipment or ignorance of safety procedures can be fatal.

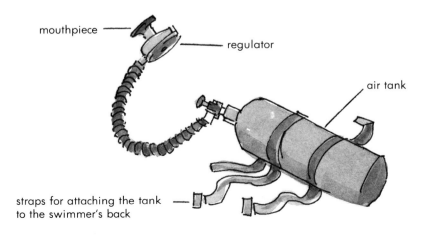

mouthpiece —

— regulator

air tank

straps for attaching the tank to the swimmer's back

Modern scuba-diving methods were developed by Jacques Cousteau. Cousteau has been responsible for countless undersea discoveries and many technical developments in diving equipment. And you have probably seen some of the movies and TV films of his underwater adventures.

As a scuba diver descends, the water pressure increases. The more depth, the more pressure. Under high pressure the chemistry of the body changes, and divers must be very careful about how they come up to the surface. Surfacing too quickly can cause a condition known as the "bends." A diver gets the bends when gas bubbles form in the bloodstream or in the body tissue. It is extremely painful and can cause paralysis and even death. Learning how to deal with the dangers of high pressure, and how to surface safely, is an important part of diver training.

During World War II scuba gear was used by navy underwater demolition teams called "frogmen." They did all sorts of stealthy, dangerous jobs, such as eliminating enemy underwater mines or planting explosives under the hulls of anchored enemy ships.

The water in an ocean, lake, or river is usually quite cold except in tropical climates. A diver wearing a protective suit such as this will be better able to endure even very cold waters.

a diver wearing a "hard hat"

Before the invention of scuba-diving equipment a lot of underwater work was done in what divers call a "hard hat." This is a rather elaborate method of diving that requires an assistant above water. The diver wears the sort of outfit shown here. The "hard hat" is made of copper and is attached to a rubberized canvas suit. Air is pumped down through a rubber hose by the assistant working an air pump. A steel cable attaches the diver to the support boat on the surface. The cable is used to raise or lower the diver. Lead weights on the feet and a heavy belt around the waist keep the diver on the sea bottom.

This is a picturesque and old-fashioned way of diving that you are more likely to see in old movies than on the scene of modern underwater activity.

Exploring the Oceans

There is still a great deal we don't know about the ocean depths. There are strange new sea creatures being discovered all the time, and the ocean bottom is as yet only partially charted. The major underwater mountain ranges have been located and the deep canyons and continental shelves are known, but there is still much to learn.

Ordinary submarines can't go deep enough to explore great depths. The *Turtle* could go down no farther than the distance of its breathing tube. World War I submarines

air hose and control
lines that are connected
to the support boat

William Beebe was one of the first deep-sea explorers. Going down a half mile in 1930 was a great accomplishment.

could rarely go down much more than 200 feet. Even modern nuclear-powered submarines will go only about 1,000 feet deep, although the exact depth to which they can go is restricted military information.

In order to go down really deep a different kind of submarine is needed. And, in fact, it is not called a submarine. It is called a submersible. A submersible is much smaller than a submarine and is not designed to travel any great distance except down. It is built to withstand deep-ocean pressures, and usually has room for no more than two or three people. Because a submersible doesn't have to move rapidly through water, it often assumes some rather strange shapes.

In 1930 a scientist by the name of William Beebe was the first man to descend as far as a half mile into the ocean depths. His submersible, which he called a bathysphere, was a heavy, hollow steel ball fitted with thick, strong windows. There was no engine, no way to navigate. The only thing that kept it from dropping like a rock to the ocean bottom was a strong steel cable. This cable, and an air-supply hose, went up to a support ship floating on the surface. Beebe and a companion discovered all kinds of deep-water creatures unknown at that time. There were iridescent jellyfish and fish with long tendrils and wispy fins, slinky sea worms, and much more that had never been seen before. Beebe's bathysphere led the way for other submersibles that eventually were able to go much deeper. Some of the modern submersibles have engines and controls so that they can travel about unconnected to surface vessels.

This submersible, the *Trieste*,
has been to the deepest part
of the ocean—35,800 feet.
The *Trieste* is made in two
parts. The upper part is like
the upper part of a hot-air
balloon. But in the *Trieste* this
part is filled with gasoline
rather than air. Gasoline is
ligher than seawater and will
not compress, so it is used
instead of air. And instead of
the basket that hangs under
the hot-air balloon there is a
strong, pressure-proof cabin in
which there is room for two or
more people.

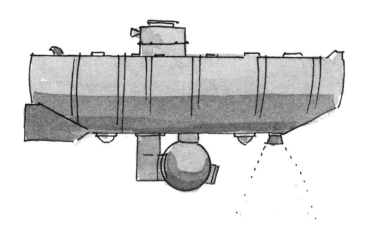

Many submarines are
designed for a specific
purpose. This one is intended
for work on underwater
pipelines.

This submersible was
developed by the
U.S. Navy and has a hatch on
the bottom that can be
attached to a sunken, disabled
submarine in order to rescue
the crew.

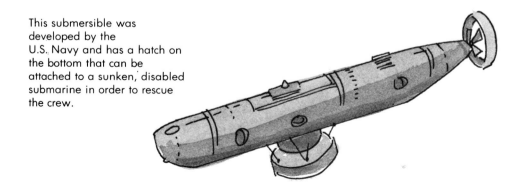

Submersibles at Work

The *Titanic* was a huge luxury ocean liner that sank on its maiden transatlantic voyage in 1912. It was considered unsinkable, but when it ran into an iceberg one dark night it did indeed sink, taking with it some 1,522 passengers and crew.

Many years later the wreck was located under 13,000 feet of water. An undersea investigation was started at

The *Titanic* wasn't aware of a field of huge icebergs until it was too late.

once to find out as much as possible about the ship: what condition it was in, how it had settled into its final resting place, and what, if anything, there was that could be salvaged. Most of this investigation was done by a submersible called the *Alvin* and its small partner called the *Jason Jr.* The *Jason Jr.* was a tethered robot with no crew.

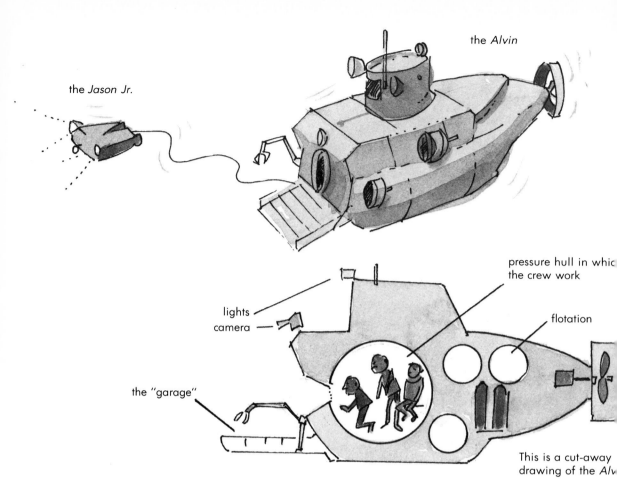

the *Jason Jr.*

the *Alvin*

pressure hull in whic[h]
the crew work

flotation

lights

camera

the "garage"

This is a cut-away
drawing of the *Al*v[in]

WOODS HOLE OCEANOGRAPHIC INSTITUTE, PHOTO BY ROD CATENACH

The *Alvin*, like many
submersibles, is being
continually modified for
special projects and to
improve its performance.

It could get into small, dangerous locations and take close-up, detailed photographs. It was attached, or tethered, to the *Alvin* by means of a long cable. Directions for its movements and picture-taking operations were controlled from inside the *Alvin*.

When the *Jason Jr.* finished its assigned tasks it was returned to a platform—called "the garage"—on the front of the *Alvin*. It remained there for the *Alvin*'s two-and-a-half-hour ascent back up to the surface and its support ship. Then the *Alvin*, along with the *Jason Jr.*, was lifted out of the water by heavy cranes.

The *Alvin* has had assignments all over the world. One of the trickiest was in 1966 when two United States aircraft collided in midair off the coast of Spain. A hydrogen bomb that one of them was carrying fell into the sea in a spot that had all sorts of underwater cliffs and canyons, and lots of mud and silt. A huge effort was made to recover the bomb. Hundreds of men and divers, and dozens of vessels of all kinds, were assembled. The *Alvin*, in the company of some other submersibles, finally managed to recover the bomb after a lot of hard work. The entire search and recovery cost four million dollars and lasted several months.

The *Alvin* is well over twenty years old now, and new and different submersibles continue to be developed. Some of the new ones are robots and do not require a crew. They are controlled through cables that connect them to surface ships. There are others that have computer programs that tell them where to go and what to do. Because there are no humans aboard these submersibles, it is possible for some of them to stay underwater indefinitely. Scientists above water sit in comfort while watching the operation by means of TV monitors.

Underwater Treasure

Submersibles or divers are needed when it comes to searching for ancient sailing vessels, sunken cities, or wrecked treasure ships. Sometimes the recovered treasure is gold and silver and precious stones. This sort of thing is, of course, of great value. But an even more important treasure is the knowledge that can be gained about old civilizations from old coins, pottery, bronze and marble statues, weapons, tools, and navigation instruments. All of these things will tell a great deal about how people lived and worked long ago.

This recovery and study of ancient, historical material from the ocean bottom is a special field called marine archaeology. It deals mainly with old shipwrecks, which can be found all over the world. The most important ones, though, have been found in the Mediterranean and in the Bahamas. Marine archaeologists examine the way old ships are constructed, the kind of cargo they carried, and other clues about the life-styles of the crew and passengers.

In the Mediterranean off the coast of Turkey, there are some dangerous waters with many jagged rocks hidden just below the surface. Many ships have been wrecked there. Some of the wrecks go back to prehistoric times, and whatever can be recovered is of great interest to achaeologists, historians, and art experts. The illustration on the opposite page shows just how a team of marine archaeologists several years ago worked on the remains of a ship that sailed in the eastern Mediterranean in the fourteenth century B.C.

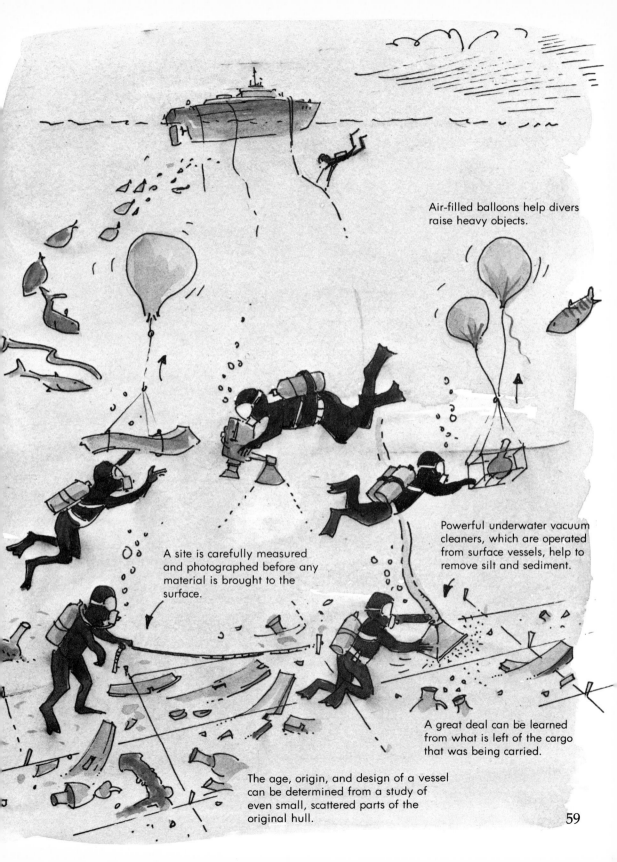

Air-filled balloons help divers raise heavy objects.

A site is carefully measured and photographed before any material is brought to the surface.

Powerful underwater vacuum cleaners, which are operated from surface vessels, help to remove silt and sediment.

A great deal can be learned from what is left of the cargo that was being carried.

The age, origin, and design of a vessel can be determined from a study of even small, scattered parts of the original hull.

Ribs, planking, and other wood parts from old sunken ships are very fragile when recovered and have to be carefully washed in fresh water and then treated with chemicals before being reassembled on dry land.

Museums all over the world display all kinds of art and artifacts that have been found on the sea bottom.

A fortune in gold, silver, and precious stones was the object of another treasure hunter's search. The experienced, professional treasure hunter spent over twenty years gathering information about the last known location of a Spanish galleon that had sunk in a storm in 1622. Using a crew of divers who searched for many years with the aid of metal-sensing instruments, the wreck of the *Atocha* was finally located off the Florida keys in 1985.

The exact value of the *Atocha*'s treasure is not yet known, but experts have estimated that it is about 200 million dollars. One item from the *Atocha,* a magnificent Renaissance gold chain, was auctioned off in 1988 for $319,000!

Commercial Operation

Many submersibles are intended for commercial operation, such as undersea mining. There are all sorts of valuable metals—iron and manganese, for example—waiting to be scooped up off the ocean floor. Other submersibles are used to help maintain oil platforms located in many parts of the world. The platform's steel supports and complicated piping are all deep underwater and have to be

A great deal of oil production apparatus is installed on the ocean floor. There are pumps and many pipes and complex operating machinery, and it must all be carefully maintained. Many divers are needed for this work.

carefully maintained. There are other submersibles that are designed for marine-research operations or for rescue missions or for maintaining ocean communication cables or for secret navy undertakings.

Some submersibles will take divers underwater and then allow them to enter or leave as needed. This kind of submersible is called a "habitat." A habitat is a place where you live—in this case an underwater "house." Divers can live in a habitat for days or weeks at a time. The advantage to this is that the divers don't have to worry about continually adjusting their bodies to the pressure of deep water. The air pressure inside the habitat is adjusted to equal the pressure of the water outside. So it is a simple matter to just put on the scuba gear and step out—or swim out—and go to work.

A habitat can be connected to a vessel on the surface.

A habitat is an underwater "house" with many of the comforts of a real house, though it wouldn't be too good an idea to try and open a window for a breath of fresh air.

OFFICIAL U.S. NAVY PHOTOGRAPH

The Future

Submarines today have reached such a state of technical perfection that it is hard to think of how improvements will be made in the future, though certainly they will be. As far as submersibles are concerned, however, new possibilities continue to appear, almost from day to day, it seems. There are still unknown depths to be explored and mapped, new archaeology sites to be investigated, marine-biology problems to deal with, and new and richer treasures to be discovered. New underwater craft for these special purposes will certainly continue to be developed.

There are several museums devoted to the submarine, both in the United States and in Europe. In Groton, Connecticut, there is the *Nautilus* Memorial Submarine Force Library and Museum. This is primarily a museum that shows the history of the submarine with many pictures and models. Most interesting is the actual, first nuclear-powered submarine, the decommissioned *Nautilus*. It is moored in the Thames River, alongside the museum, and you can go aboard and climb down and walk through a good part of this historic submarine.

Index